BARTENDING FOR A STAMP WITH MY FACE ON IT

KATE GARCIA

Chestnut Review Chapbooks, an imprint of Chestnut Review LLC
Ithaca, New York

https://chestnutreview.com
ISBN: 978-1-965158-19-7

BARTENDING FOR A STAMP WITH MY FACE ON IT

KATE GARCIA

Chestnut Review Chapbooks

Table of Contents

Bartending to be Saved

I get the job on a lie—
a matter of experience,

a matter of—
I think I've done everything wrong.

There's a spot in my kitchen,
five years older than me,

a deep, rotted pocket in the molding.
I become interested in

what might be in there—
among the spores and webbing.

I catch myself watching the pocket
as I make my coffee. I almost

stick my finger in, surrender
to the fibrous, clammy wood.

Dog walks in just in time. I take the job
to escape the pocket. I think the pocket

and me are the same. I take the job
to turn myself inside out.

I am lying
more and more these days.

Bartending from the Edge of the Pool

Things start as most things do—
with a change of the seasons,

a hair-bleaching rebirth,
a dead buck decomposing

in the neighbors' backyard,
a sudden interest in

canning fruits and vegetables,
a tax write off on ergonomic

clogs, a taste, a whiff,
a fuzzy date with

an older man, a cry for
help, a fistful of coins—

a camping trip with my ex,
a naming, a mourning,

a really big burn,
a broken bottle, a gambled

paycheck, a litter of
kittens upstairs.

A shot of Fernet, then a decision
to stay put.

Things start in the slip,
in the permission of my mother.

Bartending to Take Photos of the Fruit

Buzz asks if he can take my picture
for Facebook. He's ordered

too much food. *I have a bit of a following*
he says. *People like my reviews.*

Am I being reviewed? *No, I just think*
it'd be a good picture to include.

I have a policy. No photos. Buzz returns
to eating—chewing for too long, I think.

I arrange the fruit after cutting. Limes
then lemons then oranges then olives—

left to right. I cull the rotting,
the slimy. My camera roll is full

of close ups I think about framing—
neon green sinews and juice pockets,

the deep black border around
pimento, like a crab in its shell.

I shove condiment bottles
of simple syrup deep

into the ice well to cool—
their nipples just peeking out,

chewed up and cloudy.
The ice is burned

once a week. Sometimes twice if necessary.
Burning here is just melting.

Buzz is angling his phone over the top
of his mountain of food. Just enough

to capture my torso. I try not to stand
still. I try to blur.

Tending // March in the North Hills

From the top of the trail, I watch
two horseback riders approach

the spot I know the snakes to be.
Too far to yell, I hum a doomsday song

to Dog. I ready for the spook. Snakes
mating in the new grass, horses

gentle for their riders. I wait for the buck
from way up high.

Bartending (Because Hot People Bartend)

and I want to be hot. I want
to be hot in a girl way and a boy way.

A bot way. A seventeen-year-old way
and like my mom. So hot

that the wheels fall off—I'm out
of control! So hot I scare

the boys with my certain
special wink. Hot like an angry

spit take straight to the chest.
I want

to be hot
in a sneaky way, a decisive way,

hot enough to trust
that they talk about me

even when I'm not there.

Hot for the shame of it,
hot for the thrill of it.

I want to be
hot

in this world and the almost one—
bouncing, dream-like,

pixie-cut, peach White Claw,
fun house Lucinda,

uncomplicated, undeniable,
classic, conventional, cool

hot. Nightlight in the dark hot,
nightshade turning purple hot.

Fear not my loneliness hot—
happy and forgotten hot

at the center of the earth.

Bartending as a Family Matter

I grew in my mother while she waited tables. I grew and she ate
only prime rib and chocolate cake. I grew and she braided her hair,

saddled an apron on top of her belly where I grew. She served
Heather Locklear. While I was growing

she watched a CHP send a little old woman flying
across an intersection then drive away. She signed a petition

when asked. She made little dinner salads. I grew and she learned
how to stretch her back in a doorway after work.

My mother had never been disappointed in me
until I was 25. I have been disappointed in my mother

for centuries. I have at times thought I was the only one
growing, then shrinking, then growing. I have been disappointed

to learn that steadiness is a lie—that fear has been with us
the whole time. I think about my mother

a lot these days—about how she fell in love with angry
men. Anger can be made flat, can be draped over a life

like a sheet. I've learned that anger is bigger when wedded
to fear, when both are held in two palms of a single body.

My mother waited tables and grew me. Under an apron,
pushed up against a window of food. She mourned

the loss of her small body. I have learned that she was fearful,
that she was disappointed.

Bartending as Meditation

On a slow shift I look up the ages of everyone
        I've ever heard of. I follow all the wunderkinds who

published books at twenty-two. Someone
        orders a Colorado Bulldog. I look up how to make a

Colorado Bulldog. I read a Reddit post titled "everyone
        is ugly if you stare at them long enough." Things, too.

Places and situations. I try to keep this in mind. I try to look
        even longer, circle back around. Dog develops

a fear of water. Which proves to be warranted when
        two of his friends die of algae poisoning.

> *K: I'm the oldest I've ever been.*
> *D: Yes, but that's not the issue.*

> *K: What's the issue, then?*
> *D: General lack of discipline.*

I think about moving apartments—a place that lets
        the sunlight in. But my landlord is so nice, once

jumped my car in a blizzard when I had no one else to call. I try
        to let the sunlight in—stay big and ripe and not complain.

I stay out late one night with a man who hates his ex-wife—
        come home to find Dog has peed on the guest bed.

> *K: You're too old for this shit.*
> *D: I'm teaching you to care for things.*

I take up swimming, try to think deeply and let the water
        heave across my back. I try not to look at the other swimmers'

bodies but I can't help it—so many tiny old women swimming
        in the middle of the day. I try to gauge their levels of enjoyment—

with swimming, with life. I try to enjoy hurling my body
        back and forth, tell myself I will start masturbating

in front of a mirror. I look up Kibbe Body Typing, think
        I might swim myself all the way to gamine. I look up

the boy I fell in love with five years ago. He's never looked better.

D: I think it might help if I came to work with you.
K: Help what?

D: The Big Sad.

At the bar I feel both more and less like myself—a foreign object,
        a clump of foal feathers, wet with womb slick. I look up

the fastest way to save 4,000 dollars. I look up recipes for seed
        cycling—I try to be happier through my hormones.

I look up the article about the body my friend found floating
        in the river last fall. She described limbs twisted around

a bloated torso—a flesh mass so pale and still she thought it was snow.
        After work I stand on the bridge and watch gray chunks

of ice break off from the shore, float down the current and out of
        sight. I try not to be afraid of the water. On the phone

my mother reminds me that life takes a long time. I say
        these words back to Dog and everyone I meet or kiss or love—

10

life takes a long time. I try my best to be at the pool alone—
        too early or too late. In this hollow, tiled gourd I can float

on my back in the middle of a lane. I can snap under water, hear the glutted
        echo cup itself around my skull. Here—alone—I look up.

Bartending for the Work

Pull floormats out from where they are stacked, rinse
black grime from hands. Unplug taps, a brief beer-letting

to flush the iodine. Set up station—black bar mats branded
Tito's and *Pendleton*. I have my favorites. Boston tins, strainers,

garnish tray. Ignore the filth—fruit cut two days ago, ungloved
hands in the olive jar, greasy liquor bottle in the ice well,

a rat once. So much food—dropped behind tables, chewed
to cud and spat, stuck to the undersides of everything.

The dishwasher, edged with mold, stinking like the understory
of a sick, forgotten forest. Here, a liquor store attached to one end,

a casino to the other. Some nights, I'm in charge of it all. Here,
so much cash. Somehow, everyone has cash. Men of a certain

age. The piney smell of perfectly aged bills. Smile. Open and shut
the video poker machines when they stop working—not an

expert, the best I can do. Make the mixes, bloody and Caesar.
Bleed constantly—little nicks on fingers from Grey Goose

foil, keg swaps, going off birth control. All the men notice
when I cut my hair. Mixed responses. Money and ice, money

and ice. Bend at the hips. More. Broken nail, I'm feverish
with hangover, gag at the smell of Rumple Minze

splashed across my sinks. Make sure to pull the trash
before it gets too heavy. Or else the cross-eyed night

cook will have to help. That or a drunk Buzz.
Every morning, check the city arrest records

for DUIs. Still unclear on my level of liability.
Tell Dog everything: how that one bald guy

stayed after everyone left. Me, him,
and Cross-Eyes, daring each other

to squirm. Hot shower, steam
in the throat.

Bartending on New Year's Eve

Buzz has a girlfriend tonight. She's big and smiley—
all pinks and browns. Buzz tells me, not so quietly,

how they made love on the bubblegum bed
at the Thunderbird Motel. I am careful

with my mouth shape. I make change
for Keno, tuck ones behind ones, dirty

my fingertips with sweat and booze. Tonight,
I feel like I can't get away

with anything. Not even a cavity, let alone
a resolution. But there is beauty

in ketchup floating in dishwater,
tapped keg beer foam, the tinny plonks

of video poker machines (Buzz's girlfriend
gets into the bonus). There is beauty

in Buzz in Love, in our problems becoming
the same problems—in lust and hope and weird luck.

Tending // Late November, Miami

My garden, a fire—both
growing then shrinking.

I'm finding it hard to hold
onto little me, I'm finding

it hard to grow older
and more afraid

than I ever expected to be.
I rush toward me—

panting like an animal—
but when I open my throat

for a warning or a gift
all that comes out is

an indictment of my father,
an unanswered plea to my body,

and so much fear.
My garden, a fire—

a little dry, a little wet,
a little me waning

into someone who is okay
with being howled at.

On a trip for my friend's
30th birthday—a boat ride

over dark waters, questions
about the future

of this country, questions
about what it means

to be looked at
from the bottom

of a clouded lake—
through the

mud halo of a
cataract.

Bartending on Sunday Morning

The old couple wants me to stand at the end of their table
and laugh. I stand at the end of their table and laugh,

an apple-shaped bruise forming on my hip. I think she can tell
that I don't normally wear my hair like this, that I am concerned

about the size of my arms. The old couple tells me they're moving
next month—this state is becoming too much like California.

I think of my grandparents in California, how they'll be dying soon
and I'm so far from home. I think of the peregrine and the

moonflower. I think of Dog as a baby—of our panicky, thin bodies
rushing toward an August-crusted screen door. So much has changed.

I have become big and slow, my brain mottled, a velvet strip
of wanting that runs behind my tongue and down through my belly.

The old couple congratulates me on my schooling, finished years
ago, and asks what I will do next. I am already what is next—

waiting for a forest fire, waiting for a cartoon villain, three
drinks in and waiting for grandma to die.

Bartending from Both Sides

Buzz calls me after I get home, which scares me—
he wants to continue our conversation

about America. He tells me he is interested
in my protection—in keeping

my unborn child safe and my locker room clean.
I meet a writer who tells me he

took notes while working at a gas station—
he used them to write his novel. I try and do

the same. Everything that happens to me here
is embarrassing—the way I

smell and the things I eat. How some nights I make
five hundred dollars and some nights I make

nothing. How I say yes and yes and yes. How
I called Buzz once, too. There is a motel

across the street, lit up red as a chokecherry.
In the parking lot: me watching the men

make their phantom march. In the parking lot: me
watching petals of smoke in the lamp light.

Bartending Bacchanalia

Buzz breaks a man's arm
just as the summer sun sets

over a slow and bloated Clark Fork. The last
of the floaters return to the parking lot

when a lurid *crack* fills the valley—bounds
around the dried-up shoulders

of Mount Jumbo. There are yells
and vomit, flesh gone limp and a sour

smell ricocheting among bodies at the bar.
For a moment, I float—a bract in the wind, over

the heads of the yipping pups licking whiskey
sweat from foreheads. When I come

back down, shots abound. The boys
drape themselves over Buzz's back,

breathing heavy, tongues swollen with
terror and thrill. They are

begging—let it be them, next.

Later, I remember that time in a Seattle
bathroom when a sonic boom

rattled the bones of the building. Heart
running wild, I hid under the sinks—

waiting to be gunned down, waiting
to be shaken loose from the earth.

When I finally ventured out, prepared
to discover bloodied bomb victims,

everyone was laughing, tickled by ideas
of fighter jets and a scrambled ether.

Buzz bends his head to lick
my hand as it passes along the bar.

He looks up at me with a smile. My heart,
my heart has never slowed down.

Tending // 2AM, HWY 12

Driving home I turn toward a lunar glow
doubling the swell of the mountain. She's tucked

away, hiding her face, letting what precedes her
do the talking. If dreams meant anything

I might include this:
I'm sitting in the passenger seat of a red T100

with Buzz. He reaches up, puts a hand
to the nape of my neck,

and slowly but forcefully guides
my head down to the black hole

center of his crotch.
There's only the sound of my breathing,

the feeling of falling through
cosmic bramble, then bouncing around

the great, empty hull of a ship.
In the dream, I find myself,

I reach back, gently take his hand in mine
and place it back on the steering wheel.

I pat his cheek. *Tsk, tsk, Buzz.*
I don't feel scared. I stare straight ahead.

Now, dark umbrae on the empty road,
pine-shaped shadow boxes.

I swerve to save a field mouse, a raccoon, a
spatchcocked bag of groceries.

Really, I'm just trying
to get home. Really—

hiding, undecided,
the moon and me.

Bartending for the Days Off

Dog was a sticky puppy. Things stuck to him—
dry burrs and pine needles, memories and plans.

I spend an afternoon on mushrooms with friends—
stretched out and dazed on my couch, Dog asleep at the center

of that fluid shape our crescented bodies make.
He is a brighter shade of orange than normal, little bits

of him break off to join the winking aspen leaves outside.
I put a hand on his belly, holding him to me.

> *K: Look at you, letting go.*
> *D (groggily): Only of that which does not serve me.*

I pull him into my lap, create a new shape. I stroke the space
between his eyes, coo in his loamy ear. My little horse—

leading me back to that time in California when a goathead
pierced his paw pad, made a little hole that collected

bits of dirt, gravel. The vet dredged the hole over and over,
an endless knot of tiny detritus. Eventually—and only when left alone—

the piercing healed. Things start to fall away. I ask Dog
if he remembers the pain, even a phantom feeling. In response,

he smacks his lips, sticks his snout into my armpit. I smell
winter lifting off the carpet. I see a magpie flit the fence.

Bartending for a Stamp with My Face on It

Bartending for the little guy behind my sternum. Bartending to play make believe. Bartending for all the Keno machines in America. Bartending because the boy I like won't sleep with me. Bartending to quit the job that makes me drive. Bartending to reach my childhood home. Bartending to hear myself talk. Bartending to wear a pushup bra. Bartending to hold many truths in the palm of my hand. Bartending to hold many truths at the bottom of my glass. Bartending to give people something to look at. Bartending to sit on the floor with someone—let them take my contacts out. Bartending for a little while. Bartending to find out why all the dead elk along I-15 are missing their heads. Bartending to reasonably smoke a cigarette. Bartending to have something to do on New Year's Eve. Bartending to reach the final boss. Bartending so no one will come looking. Bartending in the pages of Cosmopolitan. Bartending for a case study. Bartending for all the men who know I'm smarter than them and want to fuck me stupid for it. Bartending in the middle of a perfectly made omelet. Bartending because it's the only thing I'm good at. Bartending to take my truck from dive to dive. Bartending because I don't believe in Botox. Bartending because, as a baby, I looked my dad in the eyes and he saw me there, brand new and wonderful and he tried so hard not to be angry with me. Bartending because I am stockpiling while I'm still young. Bartending while I am still young. Bartending to afford the tanning bed. Bartending because my big sister is going to be a lawyer. Bartending to put my phone down for a night. Bartending to drink a Red Bull. Bartending so the party never ends. Bartending to write about it. Bartending because there's bars in every city. Bartending to wear myself out. Bartending while I wait for my mom to come pick me up. Bartending to kill time. Bartending to watch NFL package for free. Bartending for work *and* for play. Bartending so that, on a November Tuesday at 10 am, I can drive along the Flathead River and watch the trumpeter swans in their little consumptions—their backsides like dusty white torches lighting up the slow current. Bartending along the Continental Divide. Bartending instead of anything else.

Tending // Late Summer, St. Ignatius

My farmer friends are gone
so I tend to their little life—open

and shut the greenhouses,
help the compost in its stinking

return, sit still for the house cat. At sunset
the light pitches pinked and clean

on the mountains. Dog lays with me
in the bluebunch while I

relish in the making of a home
that isn't mine. Tomorrow I'll return

to town, make drinks and brawl back each jutting lip but
now—now I breathe in the sour sand smell

of Montana wilting into fall,
I teethe on the world

like a baby,
like I'm brand new.

Interview with Kate Garcia

*Would you mind sharing the origins of this chapbook and how the speaker devel-
oped as you drafted these poems? Are there any key locations, characters, or experi-
ences you can point to as inspiration for this work?*

I first started writing the poems for this chapbook in late 2022. I was
post-MFA and working at a sports bar in Montana. I wasn't originally
thinking that the whole project would be so bartending focused—that
came later as I was looking back on and writing about this time in
my life. Themes started to emerge in the work and bartending kind
of revealed itself as the centerpiece of this collection. I started think-
ing a lot about how the job—both the performance of it as well as the
actual labor—had affected my sense of self, my relationship to getting
older, my relationship to the patriarchy, etc. As far as the speaker, she
is me and she's also separate from me. Through her voice I found that
I was able to tap into all these things that I've really experienced while
also leaning into a fictionalized absurdity. Dog is totally my real life
dog, Bosco.

*Your chapbook displays this beautiful balance between elevated language and vivid,
sometimes even gross, images. How would you say such a balance, or maybe even a
conflict, lends itself to the overall purpose of the chapbook?*

For me, one of the central arguments of the chapbook is that two con-
flicting truths can exist at once. The objectification that the speaker
experiences is degrading but also intoxicating. She is incredibly lonely,
but through that loneliness experiences profound freedom. The en-
vironment she finds herself in is both disgusting and beautiful. The
language in the poems, the conflict of the images, just feels true to life
for me.

Each poem tends to be grounded in series of couplets. Would you elaborate on the formal vision of your poetry? And how do mechanics such as line breaks and punctuation play a part in that vision?

To be fully transparent, writing in couplets is often less a formal "choice" for me and more just my default when drafting poems. I like putting a formal framework like that in place for myself from the onset without having to think about it. But I do love the inherent rhythm that couplets offer. I wanted the project to have some formal consistency. I found that, in the process of editing, the couplets took on more and more value in the content of the poems. For example, I think the dialogue between the speaker and Dog lends itself really well to that formal choice. As far as line breaks and punctuation, I try to just be faithful to the voice of the poem and maybe that can sometimes include a funny or surprising line break. I owe a lot to my editor, Kate, in helping me push the enjambments in this collection even further. She has an eye for line breaks that I have not been blessed with.

There are a few key characters in your work that take on almost archetypal roles. What does the presence of Buzz, Dog, and maybe any other informal characters provide for the speaker's experience and the readers' witness of it?

For me, the three central characters of this collection (the speaker, Dog, and Buzz) are a kind of symbiotic triangle. Dog gets to be the stand in for all the ways in which the speaker is trying to be faithful to her own values. He represents the safety of the domestic space. He represents real, transformative love—love that encourages the speaker to be a better version of herself. Buzz, on the other hand, is the embodiment of danger, patriarchy, sexual violence, etc. I created Buzz as a kind of composite of all the bar patrons I'd had the experience of interacting with. I hope the reader can feel how both archetypes are important to this speaker's experience moving through the world, growing up.

I'm currently at work on my first full-length manuscript, which includes themes I've been interested in since my MFA. They're poems about my family, California, wildfires, and quilting—all things that feel pretty central to who I am as a poet and as an artist. I'm hoping to have the project near complete by the end of this year.

Acknowledgements

I am endlessly grateful to the following publications, where versions of these poems first appeared:

Fugue: "Bartending to be Saved" (published as "Bartending as Functionally Equivalent Replacement Behavior")
phoebe: "Bartending (Because Hot People Bartend)"
The Florida Review: "Bartending as a Family Matter"
Iron Horse Literary Review: "Bartending as Meditation"
The Boiler: "Bartending for a Stamp with My Face on It"

I also need to thank my family for their endless and enthusiastic support. These poems would not exist without it. And to my favorite poets—Claire, Mark, Nik, Sabrina, and Sam—for being instrumental in the shaping of this project.

About the Author

Kate Garcia is a poet from the Inland Empire of Southern California and a graduate of University of Montana's MFA program. Her poems have appeared in *Gulf Coast Journal, Florida Review, Fugue* and elsewhere.